ANCIENT EGYPT

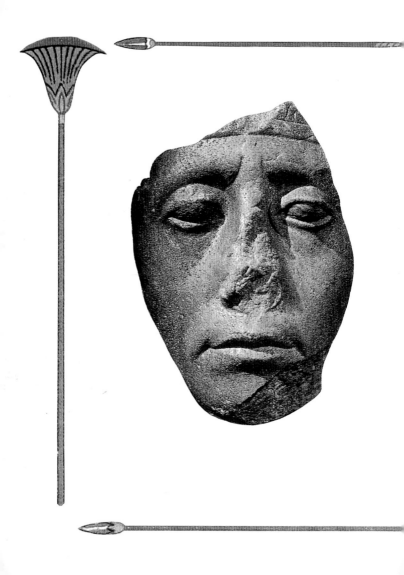

ANCIENT WISDOM
FOR THE NEW AGE

ANCIENT EGYPT

Zelda Sharif

NEW
HOLLAND

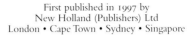

First published in 1997 by
New Holland (Publishers) Ltd
London • Cape Town • Sydney • Singapore

24 Nutford Place
London W1H 6DQ
UK

80 McKenzie Street
Cape Town 8000
South Africa

3/2 Aquatic Drive
Frenchs Forest, NSW 2086
Australia

ISBN 1 85368 949 1 (hb)

DESIGNED AND EDITED BY
Complete Editions
40 Castelnau
London SW13 9RU

EDITORIAL DIRECTION: Yvonne McFarlane
EDITOR: Michèle Brown
DESIGNER: Peter Ward

Reproduction by Modern Age Repro House Ltd, Hong Kong
Printed and bound in Singapore by Tien Wah Press Pte Ltd

This is a gift book. It is not inteded to encourage diagnosis
and treatment of illnesses, disease or other general problems by the
layman. Any application of the recommendations set out in the
following pages is at the reader's discretion and sole risk.

CONTENTS

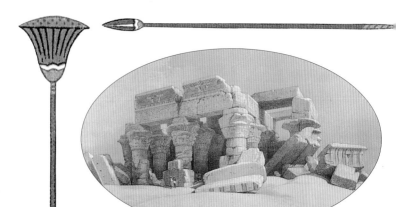

ACROSS THE MILLENIA

Herodotus wrote in the 5th century BC that 'Ancient Egypt has to show more wisdom and wonders than those of any land, and works of architecture beyond expression great'. The pharaohs were the greatest line of rulers in the history of the world, even greater than the emperors of China. It is not surprising in view of their vast legacy that they should be an endless source of fascination.

Compared to other great empires, ancient Egypt seems a gentle and optimistic place. Civil order was based on religious faith, rather than a system of laws and punishments. Even when engaged in conquest, there was no gratuitous killing or unnecessary cruelty.

Where the oldest deities originated we can never know, but we can date the earliest dynasties of pharaohs. In 3000 BC the first pharaoh unified the Upper and Lower Kingdoms of Egypt, founded the city of Memphis and began the development of hieroglyphics. The first great stone structures, mesmerizing ever since, were built around 2500 BC, necessitating warfare to plunder neighbouring

countries for building materials. From this age we still marvel at the Great Pyramid and Great Sphinx at Giza.

There followed a period of internal strife until the pharoahs at Thebes re-unified the country. By 1700 BC the horse-drawn chariot helped Egypt regain lost land. With the coming of the New Kingdom in 1570 BC, many great pharoahs reigned; Hatshepsut built her temple at Deir-el-Bahri, Amenhotep III founded the great complex at Luxor. Religious upheaval was caused by

Akhenaten, who allowed the worship of only one god. Then the boy-king, Tutankhamun, reigned for twelve years. Embalmed and buried with his treasures, he was gloriously resurrected when his tomb was found 3000 years later. Rameses III built the great Abu Simbel

temple in 1195 BC, bringing this dynasty to an end. Egypt once again fell apart and tomb robbing began. From the 25th dynasty Egypt was invaded and ruled by foreign kings, but enjoyed artistic and cultural rebirth, through the injection of foreign blood. Alexander the Great ruled for nine years from 332 BC, but spent only a few months in the

country. He was followed, from 355 BC, by the Greek Ptolemies. Their 250-year reign ended with the infamous Cleopatra and her son by Julius Caesar, Caesarion, who was murdered. Painted portraits show the Egyptians being assimilated into the Roman world, both in looks and culture.

We can only conjecture the thoughts of the ancient pharoahs. So many carved inscriptions recording their philosophy, rituals and conquests were ruthlessly erased by successive pharaohs to promote their own names and fame. The elusive mysteries of the ancient Egyptians still fascinate across the millenia. We can profit from their greatness by an intuitive understanding of their culture and its background.

II

GIFT OF THE NILE

The life-blood of ancient Egypt was the great river Nile. It flows almost 4,200 miles (6760 km) from its main source in Lake Victoria, through the ancient kingdom of Kush, north-wards through Upper Egypt to the first cataract and  Aswan, then through Lower Egypt, before reaching the delta at modern-day Cairo.

The Nile valley is a fertile, narrow strip surrounded by inhospitable desert. The fortunes of the early Nile dwellers depended upon the river's inexorable cycle of three seasons; Inundation, Emergence of the Fields and Harvest. They did not know that the annual surge of water was the

melted snow of the Ethiopian highlands, but believed that
it welled up from great caverns below the Nubian desert.
Under the aegis of the god Thoth, the first solar calendar
was invented to predict the arrival of these all-important
seasons. Stone markers were erected near the first cataract
to measure the Nile's flow. To maximize the use of the
water an extensive system of irrigation ditches and dikes
was constructed, which remained in use until the arrival of
modern flood-control techniques and dams.

The gift of the Nile was not its great abundance, but the regularity of the seasons. Neighbouring countries with regular rainfall were said to have 'a Nile in the skies'.

The Nile was more than a source of sustenance. It was the basis of all the beliefs and actions of the ancient Egyptians. The Nile gods were depicted with pendulous breasts, representing fertility, fecundity and the cycle of life. The Nile influenced the death rituals of the ancient Egyptians and their expectations in the afterlife. From centuries past

we receive their message of unquestioning belief, and trust,
in the forces of Nature.

GLORIOUS SUN

The relentless sun dominated ancient Egyptian philosophy, theology and everyday life. Without it the Egyptians knew that there could be no life. With the sun came prosperity and, when the Nile waters did not inundate the land, adversity. The sun naturally mummified their dead before they developed sophisticated methods of evisceration, anointing and bandaging to preserve bodies for eternal life.

The sun was Re, the personification of the solar disc. He was joined as a sun god by the scarab, Khepri, in the morning and by Atum in the evening. In later years each hour was given a minor deity or symbol; a child for the

first and second hours, a monkey shooting an arrow for the seventh hour, symbolizing the strong, midday rays of the run. Soaring birds such as the falcon and the kite were also associated with the sun.

Atum reigned at Heliopolis. He brought forth Shu and Tefnet, air and water, the stuff of life. They produced Geb, the earth god and Nut, the sky. Their children were Osiris, Isis, Seth and Nephthys, making up the principal pantheon of nine gods.

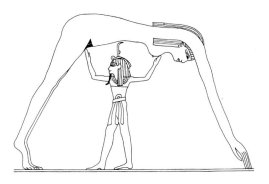

SHU and NUT: Shu, the god of air, is often shown separating Nut (sky) from Geb (earth).

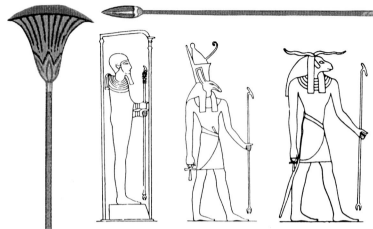

PTAH: Creator-god of Memphis, where he stood in place of Amun. Patron god of craftsmen, embodied in Greek myth as Hephaestus, bringer of fire.

SETH: Killer of his brother, Osiris, he was the god of storms and violence, embodied in Greek myth as Typhon – hence, typhoon.

KHNUM: The 'father of fathers, mother of mothers', was the ram-headed god who moulded man on a potter's wheel.

BES: A dwarf-deity, he was a protective, domestic god and helper of women during childbirth.

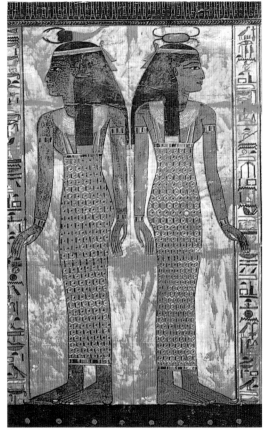

Of all the metals and precious stones used to adorn the pharaohs, gold was predominant. It was dedicated to the sun god, Re, whose cartouche or symbol describes him as 'the mountain of gold who radiates the world'. The gold images of Tutenkhamun glowed as new when his tomb was unsealed by Lord Carnarvon and Howard Carter in 1922. Death masks and furniture were heavily gilded. Its immutability made it a natural symbol of life after death. Its lasting attributes are proved by its continuing use today, 4000 years after it was fashioned into wondrous objects for the pharaohs.

SCARAB SUN

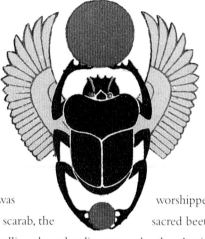

The sun was worshipped in the form of a scarab, the sacred beetle. It is depicted rolling the solar disc across the sky. Ancient Egyptians thought that the beetle emerged from the ball of dung it rolled up and down hills. So, the black dung-beetle was worshipped as the god Khepri, meaning 'he who came forth from the earth' and was seen as the image of self-creation. From earliest times, he was equated with Atum as a form of the sun god with life-enhancing gifts.

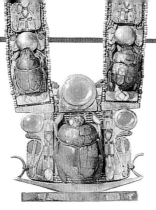

Many scarab pendants, brooches, paintings and carvings survive. When worn they were thought to induce light and warmth. Made from soapstone, glazed earthenware or gemstones, often in elaborate gold settings, they were placed in tombs as a symbol of renewed life. Yet again, a macabre living creature, such as the vulture or the jackal, was transformed by the ancient Egyptians into a positive life force which remains potent today.

23

ONE GOD

The pharaoh Akhenaten sings of the sun-god's attributes in his lyrical *Hymn to the Sun*

> *How manifold are all thy works*
> *They are hidden before us.*
> *Oh thou sole god, whose powers*
> *no other possesseth.*

Amenophis IV (c. 1375 BC) changed his name to Akhenaten, Incarnation of the Sun God, when he pronounced that there should be only one god in Egypt – Aten, the Sun Disc. All other deities, however ancient and regional, were banned and the sun became the sole god, creator and sustainer. He built a new city at Tell-el-Armana, City of the Horizon of

the Sun, and attempted to erase signs of the old religion. It was only a partial success, as the priestly caste looked upon his move as weakening their power. He reigned, with his wife, Nefertiti, for seventeen years, but his new religion barely outlasted him. Soon after his death the boy king, Tutenkhamun, revived the old religion with the old gods being returned to their shrines.

But Akhenaten had handed down to us the first concept of a single god, a concept which would eventually influence Christianity and other religions.

OSIRIS

The greatest god of the ancient Egyptians was Osiris. In antiquity he was thought to have been a humane ruler, teaching man the arts of civilization and agriculture. He introduced vine- and corn-growing and was a symbol of fertility. In this capacity he was aided by the god, Min, who is often depicted beside a stylized lettuce, a powerful aphrodisiac, the effects of which are always obvious (*see right*).

Osiris was husband to his sister, Isis, through whose magical powers he became ruler of the underworld. His brother, Seth, jealous of his popularity, enticed him into a chest, which he threw into the Nile. Isis eventually found the body, but left it unattended. Seth took advantage of this and cut it into fourteen pieces which he scattered about Egypt. Isis searched for them and, when she found them all, had Anubis bind them in bandages, like a mummy. In the form of a falcon,  she beat her wings bringing life to the inert Osiris. He was unable to return to earth and was installed as the god of the dead, proof that there was life after death.

His drowning became a symbol of rebirth, associated with the flooding of the Nile; his power demonstrated by the sprouting of vegetation. Seeds trodden in by pigs symbolized Seth killing Osiris; their sprouting, rebirth. To encourage fertility, an image of Osiris was fashioned from mud and implanted with grains. Their germination represented the unconquerable nature of life. Such charms were still in use, even in Europe, well into the 19th century.

Of all the ancient Egyptian deities, Isis was worshipped longest, well into the age of Cleopatra. Suppliants crowded into her temple at Philae. As wife and sister of Osiris, and mother of Horus, she was the embodiment of both the throne and motherhood. Her headdress, the sun disc held by a cow's horns, reflects these attributes. She was imbued with magical powers of healing and protection, at times with the dark aspect of vengeance. Together with her sister, Nephthys, she pro-tected the dead on earth in their sarcophagi. Her spells were meaningful to ordinary Egyptians; for child-birth, crocodile

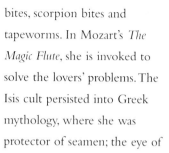

bites, scorpion bites and tapeworms. In Mozart's *The Magic Flute*, she is invoked to solve the lovers' problems. The Isis cult persisted into Greek mythology, where she was protector of seamen; the eye of her son, Horus, is still painted on Mediterranean fishing boats. She is with us today, as the High Priestess of the Tarot and hovers protec-

THE HIGH PRIESTESS

tively over us as the constellation Sirius, alongside Osiris as Orion.

MYSTICAL ANIMALS

Animal cults existed before the age of the great gods, such as Osiris and Isis. Their symbolism was absorbed by these gods, who often appeared in animal form, thereby acquiring their magical qualities.

The GOOSE represented the egg-creation myth, being sacred to Amun, who is often portrayed as this bird. The PHOENIX was inspired by the vision of the elegant heron rising out of the Nile waters as the sun's first rays flashed across their surface. It represents the sun god, Re, and the cycle of rising and setting, renewing itself after a fiery death. The SNAKE was both worshipped and feared. Apophis was threatening, but Mehen helped the sun god through the darkness of night. As a circular symbol, biting its own tail, it is a symbol of protection. Because snakes shed their old skin, they were a symbol of survival after death.

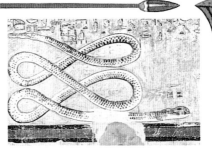

The fleeting white ANTELOPE was worshipped as the goddess Satis, the 'lady of Elephantine', who dispensed the cool water of one of the Nile cataracts. The HARE's swiftness represented heightened awareness and acute senses.

The soaring flight of the FALCON was the symbol of the soul, while their wings protected the earth. BEES were the tears of the great god, Re, as honey was important for health and beauty.

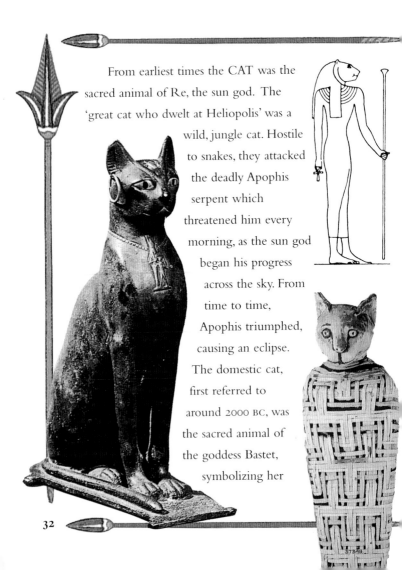

From earliest times the CAT was the sacred animal of Re, the sun god. The 'great cat who dwelt at Heliopolis' was a wild, jungle cat. Hostile to snakes, they attacked the deadly Apophis serpent which threatened him every morning, as the sun god began his progress across the sky. From time to time, Apophis triumphed, causing an eclipse. The domestic cat, first referred to around 2000 BC, was the sacred animal of the goddess Bastet, symbolizing her grace. Models of cats were proferred at her temple so that the donor might share Bastet's grace. Thousands of mummified cats were accorded burials around her temple. A mystical animal of the night, it was also worshipped for its mouse-catching ability.

The APE was associated with the god Thoth, the patron of scribes and inventor of heiroglyphics.

BABOONS watched over Thoth's shoulder as he wrote down the result of the 'weighing of the heart' in the afterlife.

The JACKAL, representing Anubis, god of the dead conducts that ceremony.

The IBIS was a reincarnation of Thoth and were specially bred to be embalmed and offered at his temples.

The BULL was a potent fertility symbol and represented the inundation of the Nile, which made the land fertile. The Bull of Apis was the most influential oracle, consulted by pharaohs and nobles. The COW, associated with the joy of Hathor and the fecundity of Isis, also symbolized fertility and birth. The sky goddess, Nut, was thought to have taken the form of a PIG and devoured her children, the stars. But each evening they were re-born, making it a symbol of fertility. The RAM, associated with Amun, was another such symbol.

Generally the Pig was regarded as unclean, as it is to this day in lands surrounding what was ancient Egypt. It was associated with Seth, who attacked Horus in the guise of a black boar. FISH were also unclean and were not eaten by the nobility and priests. It was thought that they had eaten parts of the dismembered body of Osiris. The CROCODILE was the embodiment of the evil god, Seth, and was killed alongside him by Horus to avenge the death of his father.

THE PYRAMIDS

'*The Great Pyramid whose pure and perfect surface of blameless stone, eschews every thought of idolatry and sin.*'

Charles Piazzi Smyth

Astronomer Royal for Scotland, 1845

The Great Pyramid at Giza is a timeless reminder of the mysteries of the ancient Egyptians. Over the centuries its

deepest significance has been sought after by philosophers, mathematicians and astronomers. Sir Isaac Newton thought that its dimensions might reveal the circumference of the earth; others believed it could be used to calculate the distance to the sun. The King's Chamber was thought to be the standard measure of capacity for all nations. As an observatory, its long tunnels may have been primitive telescopes for the 'watchers of the night' to chart the skies.

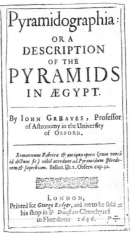

Pyramidographia:
OR A
DESCRIPTION
OF THE
PYRAMIDS
IN ÆGYPT.

By IOHN GREAVES, Professor
of Astronomy in the University
of OXFORD.

*Romanorum Fabricæ & antiqua opera (cum venia
id dictum sit) nihil accedunt ad Pyramidum splendo-
rem, & superbiam. Bellon. lib.2, Observ. cap.42.*

LONDON,
Printed for *George Badger*, and are to be sold at
his shop in St. *Dunstan* Churchyard
in Fleet-street 1 6 4 6.

One theory states that the Great Pyramid was built, not by Egyptians, but by the priests of Atlantis, to house their wisdom and treasures, in anticipation of the engulfing of their city by the sea.

In the centuries since it was built, many have sought meaning in the mathematics of its construction. Faith was put into numbers; the five sides and five points represented the five senses; or the measurements so divided as to give the date of creation as 4004 BC. The mysteries of pyramid construction remain, and play a part in contemporary Masonic rituals.

The shape of the pyramid was thought to have been inspired by the downward rays of the all-powerful sun. Their power, concentrated at the peak of the pyramid, was thought to produce cosmic forces within. In the darkness, plants flourished; in the damp atmosphere, animals were desiccated and mummified.

Pyramid Power was propounded by the 20th-century occult master, Aleister Crowley. He spent his honeymoon night in the King's Chamber, reporting increased sexual prowess, in spite of the stone floor. Using improvised pyramids, or pyramids indicated by their five designated points, it is claimed that the atmosphere created can calm children and help sleep, ease pre-menstrual tension and sharpen the senses. They are also said to keep razor blades sharp.

The ultimate mystery of the pyramids can never be unlocked, but if the hopes of the great pyramidologists were realized, modern man would be united with the collected wisdom of the ancients.

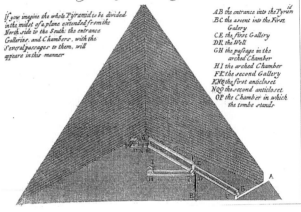

The inside of the first and fairest Pyramid

If you imagine the whole Pyramid to be divided
in the midst of a plane extended from the
North side to the South; the entrance
Galleries, and Chambers, with the
several passages to them, will
appeare in this manner

AB the entrance into the Pyramid
BC the ascent into the First
   Galery
CE the first Gallery
DR the Well
GH the passage in the
   arched Chamber
HI the arched Chamber
FK the second Gallery
KNQ the first anticloset
NQO the second anticloset
OP the Chamber in which
   the tombe stands

ANCIENT EGYPT AND
THE TAROT

In the 18th century many theories existed about the
origin of the Tarot cards. Court de Gebelin, a French
writer who specialized in myth and legend, believed that
the Tarot was the condensed wisdom of the ages, rescued

after the Great Library at Alexandria was burned down. The twenty-two 'face' cards represented the temporal and spiritual leaders of ancient Egyptian society. The fifty-six other cards were divided into four suits, representing the four classes of ancient Egyptian society, with their symbols. The King and military carried the sword, the priesthood, the cup, farmers, the baton or club, and those engaged in commerce, the coin.

The occultist, Ettiella, believed that the originals of the Tarot had been drawn on gold leaves at a Temple of Memphis, whilst others thought that the images of the twenty-two main cards would be found painted on a subterranean gallery in the Great Pyramid at Giza. Modern archaeology has found no such evidence. The goddess, Isis, lives on as the High Priestess of the modern Tarot.

SECRETS OF THE SPHINX

The Great Sphinx at Giza is one of the deepest enigmas bequeathed by the ancient Egyptians. It is a represents an image of the pharaoh, Chephren, in 2540 BC, embodying his royal power and authority. In antiquity, it was suffused with magical powers. One papyrus tells how, when the young prince Tuthmosis fell asleep between its outstretched paws, he heard the Sphinx promise him the throne of Egypt if he cleared away the sand in which it had become submerged in over the centuries. He did so, and reigned for seven years, a thousand years after the Sphinx was carved.

The Egyptian sphinx is a benevolent image, acting as a fatherly guardian, unlike the malevolent Greek sphinx, usually female in form. At Thebes, she sat at the crossroads asking a riddle. Those who did not know the answer were killed and eaten by her.

The sphinx is symbolic of everything mysterious and enigmatic. Its inscrutable face and calm expression make it a good focus for meditation, inducing a similar sense of tranquillity within the meditator.

SISTERHOOD

Ancient Egypt led the way in giving full status to women; from servants to monarchs, their position in society was more advanced than that of their sisters in 19th-century Europe and America. They could buy and sell goods and inherit property, as well as having a legally binding share of their husbands worldly goods.

There are no records of marriage ceremonies, but marriage contracts exist which, if followed to the letter, would have made Egyptian men the most considerate in history. Tales of loving marriages are legion, such as that between Tutankhamun and Ankhesenamon. Many tender letters, in which men address their wives as 'sister', encouraged the belief that incestuous marriages were common. In fact, it was a term of endearment; marrying siblings was mostly confined to the ruling houses.

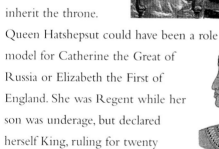

Women could inherit the throne. Queen Hatshepsut could have been a role model for Catherine the Great of Russia or Elizabeth the First of England. She was Regent while her son was underage, but declared herself King, ruling for twenty years. Being King rather than Queen, she is often depicted wearing the traditional kingly beard.

BEAUTY RITES

The ancient Egyptians were particularly creative in the arts of body and facial decoration. Styles and patterns were rigidly adhered to, indicating status in society. Many unguents were applied to guard against the dry climate of the Nile valley. Perfumes were widely used for sensual effect, not to mask body odours, as was the case in medieval Europe.

Honey and beeswax featured in many of the unguents. As a fashion accessory they were shaped into cones for

women to wear on their heads during banquets. As the proceedings and the hall warmed up the wax would

slowly melt and release exotic aromas. Ash, for its abrasive qualities was used in soaps, pre-dating similar oatmeal concoctions popular today. Myrrh was the most highly-prized aromatic oil, used as a body perfume to help avoid skin irritations.

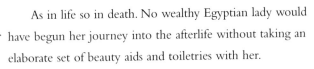

As in life so in death. No wealthy Egyptian lady would have begun her journey into the afterlife without taking an elaborate set of beauty aids and toiletries with her.

Make-up spoons and palettes, often of female shape, together with bone combs, cosmetic jars and polished mirrors, ensured their immaculate appearance before the gods.

Hairstyles were elaborate and involved complicated plaiting and interweaving with jewels and pottery beads, fashions which have not dated. Artificial hair pieces were used to create fantastic shapes and wigs were commonly used for decoration as well as signs of rank and class. Young men wore sidelocks which, when on royal heads, were the mark of a crown prince.

Many of the queens of Egypt are regarded as beauty icons, Nefertiti, being the supreme example. They were for ever beautiful as, once depicted in the prime of youth, their image remained unchanged for the rest of their life. Their sculpted profiles and dramatically coloured faces, enhanced with henna or by kohl mixed with ground gemstones, are inspiration for make-up styles today.

MEDICINE OR MAGIC

Medicine and magic, as with all early societies, were inevitably linked, though the ancient Egyptians were skilful at dealing with physiological problems and external wounds. Intricate surgery was practised on the brain. Balms and potions were formulated to aid the healing process. The ancient Egyptians were also the first to realize and record the importance of the pulse, which they called the 'voice of the heart'.

Relying on natural resources, ancient Egyptians paralleled the Chinese in the use of homeopathic remedies, but unlike the Chinese were not aware of doing so. Theirs was an instinctive belief in nature. They mixed Nile mud into potions which proved effective in healing wounds, believing this was because the Nile represented rebirth. They did not know that the antibiotic aureomycin is one of its constituents.

Shaving of head and body hair was also practised, particularly of army recruits, as a routine hygiene precaution.

An intriguing papyrus describes the use of clear Nile water in which mould can be seen to 'swim' as an effective antibiotic. Could they have unwittingly discovered penicillin'?

A papyrus of 3,600 years ago pre-dates our own knowledge of the properties of honey. Of a thousand remedies listed, over half involve this foodstuff. It can

soothe a wound and speed healing, particularly of broken skin. Its constituent hydrogen peroxide cleanses the wound, whilst it has the ability to absorb water and so dry wounds. There are records of one of the first contraceptive jellies, concocted from honey and acacia. Honey was thought to be the active ingredient but, in fact, oil of acacia spikes is deadly to sperm.

The ancient Egyptians' use of natural remedies and their trust in the inherent goodness of nature has come full circle, with our own increasing belief in holistic and homeopathic treatments today.

To calm coughs and moisten dried lungs (afflictions commonly aggravated by the Nilotic weather conditions) take one dried fig, one date, a sprinkling of aniseed and a teaspoon of honey. Cover with a little water and simmer until the fruits are tender and the liquid has become a shiny syrup.

SACRED SYMBOLS

The ancient Egyptian language possessed only a single word for 'writing' and 'drawing', which explains the close connection between script and image. These symbols inspire ideas for pendants and other ornaments which many people still wear for their secret power.

The ANKH sign, held by the goddess Ma'at in this cartouche, represents the essential life force. It signified the eternal existence of the gods and had the attributes of air and water, the very stuff of life. An ankh is easily moulded in clay or made of interwoven wire threads. When worn on a strap, as an anklet, it may help relieve ailments of legs and feet.

The simple SA sign, taken from a heiroglyph representing a herdsman's rolled up papyrus shelter, is another symbol of protection. It is associated with the goddess of childbirth and can be attached to beds of prospective mothers.

PAPYRUS, used to make the earliest paper, also symbolized the world rising from primeval waters. Columns based on its image were a permanent reminder of its emergence from the flooded Nile. It came to represent 'becoming green' or 'flourishing'.

The DJED is a fetish from pre-historic times. In its most stylized form it is the backbone of the god Osiris, symbolizing his ultimate victory over his killer, Seth. It was used in fertility rites, when the djed pillar was ritualistically raised by the pharaoh and his priests.

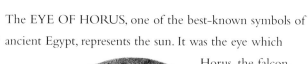

The EYE OF HORUS, one of the best-known symbols of ancient Egypt, represents the sun. It was the eye which Horus, the falcon-headed god, gave to his father, Osiris after he was murdered by his brother, Seth. It represents generosity of heart and mind; a quality to be encouraged.

The TET symbol is similar in form to the ankh and is thought to be based on the knot in the girdle worn by the gods. Carved out of a reddish semi-precious stone, such as a garnet, it was often placed with a mummy as protection on the journey through the afterlife. It can still create a protective aura.

KA is the symbol of male
potency, meaning 'bull'. Its
symbol of upraised arms
reflecting a bull's horns. This is a
defensive gesture to preserve the

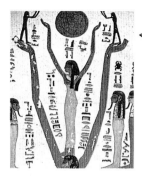

life of the
wearer from
evil. The ka
accompanied a person from birth to death
and went to the netherworld in symbolic
form, representing sustenance in the form of food offerings.

The RING is the symbol of eternity,
often held by gods such as Heh,
whose name means 'a million'.
Divine animals held the symbol
in their claws or wings, adding
to their special powers and
influences. It gives protection
from illness or physical adversity.

SACRED STONES

All Nature was sacred to the ancient Egyptians. Even the rock into which they carved their inscriptions had a place in the magical and religious universe. Particular gems and stones have a special place in their mysteries.

Malachite, an ore of copper, with its various rich green shades had a natural fascination. Green was the colour of joy, identified with Hathor, the goddess of music, dance and love. Inscriptions call her the Lady of the Malachite. The Field of Malachite was the dwelling place of the blessed, suggesting that a malachite ornament can impart a joyous and trouble-free atmosphere.

Lapis lazuli was one of the most-used precious stones in head-dresses, amulets and pendants. The Vulture Pendant, above, was found around the neck of the mummy of Tutankhamun. Deep blue with gold speckles, lapis was seen as an image of the starry sky. Blue was associated with Amun, the primeval creator god. Regalia made of lapis lazuli placed the wearer under the protection of the sun and the heavens. Judges wore amulets of it, engraved with the word 'truth' to guide their judgments. Wearing it emphasizes mystical qualities and clarity of mind.

GLORIOUS AFTERLIFE

The ancient Egyptians' attitude to death and the afterlife was positive. Resigned to the inevitability of death, they regarded the trip to 'the Land of the West', where the sun sets, as a continuation of life. A sign of their contentment

with life on earth – and their reluctance to leave it – was the considerable effort they made to replicate it in the afterlife.

Elaborate preparations were made for the journey and the final resting place. Everyday necessities, from furniture to food, were taken for the long journey. Carvings of servants, ushabti figures, were taken to serve their masters. Food had

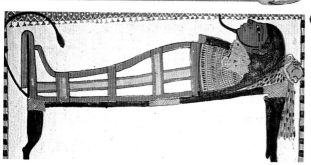

to be prepared to sustain the ka, or spiritual double, which guarded the embalmed body. Animals, particularly cats, were also embalmed to make the journey alongside their earthly owner.

Bodies were embalmed, as preservation was essential for survival after death. This ritual taking as long as seventy days. Each organ was accorded a guardian god to ensure additional protection. During the ritual, passages from *The Book of the Dead* were recited, the book being buried to serve as a guide on the last journey.

The morality of the ancient Egyptians was based on a firm social code handed down by the gods, who would

ultimately judge standards of ethics in the afterlife. After death the heart, representing good and bad actions, was weighed against the feather of truth from the headdress of the goddess Ma'at. She embodied the concept of law, truth and world order. Judges were priests of Ma'at, upholding the laws handed down by the gods.

The jackal-headed god of embalming, Anubis, did the weighing, whilst the ibis-headed Thoth, inventor of heiroglyphics, recorded the result. The god of the afterlife, Osiris, with whom the dead were identified, dispensed judgement. If it went against the deceased, the terrible creature, Amemit, part crocodile, leopard and hippopotamus waited to devour him. The scales remain a symbol of justice today.

ACKNOWLEDGMENTS

Illustrations are from the Metropolitan Museum and
Brooklyn Museum, New York, the Huntingdon Library,
San Marino, California, the Agyptisches Museum, Berlin,
the Cairo Museum, the Dictionary of Egyptian Ornament,
the Corcoran Collection and Grapharchive.
The publishers have made every effort to identify all
illustration sources. Any errors and omissions will be
corrected in future editions.